**Genre** Realistic Fiction

 **Essential Question**
What motivates you to accomplish a goal?

by Vivienne Joseph
illustrated by Roger Harvey

Chapter 1
A Jungle?.............................2

Chapter 2
I'm Really Sorry.......................5

Chapter 3
On Safari............................9

Chapter 4
Breaking Free!.......................12

Respond to Reading...............16

PAIRED READ Just for Once..............17

Focus on Literary Elements........20

Chapter 1
A JUNGLE?

"Hi, Mom, I'm home!" Ethan called. He signed to her as well, because Mom was hearing impaired.

"Hi, honey," she replied. She put a snack on the table. "You need to clean up your room today."

"What's wrong with my room?"

"Ethan, it's like a jungle in there. I'm surprised that wild animals don't live in there."

"I know there are piles of stuff lying around," he said, "but there aren't any animals."

Ethan opened the door. Books and papers covered his desk, and socks peeked out from under his bed.

His mom said his room was like a jungle, but Ethan knew where everything was—well, mostly.

Ethan opened his schoolbag, and looked through the jumble of books and papers. Suddenly, he remembered the book **presentation**. He had to talk about a book in front of his class tomorrow. Then he remembered the library book that he needed to return. Where was it?

Ethan looked under his bed.

Ethan wriggled under the bed on his stomach. All he could see were dust bunnies. He was crawling out when his older brother, Joe, came in.

"Is your homework going okay?"

"It's fine," Ethan replied.

Joe said, "Let me know if you need any help."

Ethan looked around and sighed. The library book must be in his closet. He took a deep breath and opened the closet door.

Suddenly, a stack of board games crashed down from the top shelf. Then Ethan noticed something in the corner of the closet—his library book!

"Yes!" he said. But when Ethan opened the book, he saw that it was **overdue**. He should have returned it weeks ago.

STOP AND CHECK

Why is Ethan's room like a jungle?

Chapter 2
I'M REALLY SORRY

The next morning, Ethan practiced his presentation. "I've finally **memorized** my presentation, so I can do it without my notes," he told his mom.

"You can return your library book after school." Then his mom saw the due date. "This book is really overdue!"

"Sorry, Mom. I couldn't find it."

"Ethan," his mom said, "you have to take **responsibility** for organizing your room."

When he arrived at school, Ethan saw Blake and Luis. "Did you bring your part of our science project?" Blake asked.

"That's not due until next week," Ethan replied.

"No, it's due today," Blake said.

Luis sighed, "Mr. Wong won't be happy. He doesn't like projects to be late."

"I'm sorry—you should have texted me," Ethan said.

"It's not my fault you forgot," Blake said.

The three boys went to see Mr. Wong.

"I'm sorry, Mr. Wong. It's my fault we haven't finished the project," Ethan admitted. He felt embarrassed, and he started to blush.

"You need to be more organized, Ethan," Mr. Wong said. He gave Ethan a serious look.

After class, Ethan asked Luis, "The book presentation is due today, right?"

"That's next week," said Luis.

That afternoon Mr. Wong asked Ethan for his permission slip for the field trip.

"Sorry, Mr. Wong, but it's at home somewhere," said Ethan.

Mr. Wong looked angry. "If you don't hand it in tomorrow, you can't come on the trip."

Ethan felt sick. Nothing was going right.

After school, Ethan **trudged** slowly to the bus with Blake.

"Do you want to go skateboarding?" Blake asked.

Ethan thought about the science project and the permission slip that was lost in the jungle of his room. "I can't today," he said, "but maybe tomorrow?"

"We've got practice tomorrow after school," said Blake. "You've got that in your planner, right?"

Ethan nodded. But he had no idea where his planner was.

STOP AND CHECK

What things happen because Ethan is not organized?

Chapter 3
ON SAFARI

"I made muffins," Ethan's mom said when he arrived home. "How did your book presentation go?"

"Yum!" said Ethan, taking a bite of his muffin so he couldn't reply. When he finished eating, Ethan went to his room.

"I'll renew your library book tomorrow," his mom said. "You can pay the fine out of your allowance."

"Okay," Ethan called. But nothing was okay. He thought about everything that went wrong today. He worried about paying the **massive** library fine. It was a lot of money!

STOP AND CHECK

Why doesn't Ethan tell his mom about the book presentation?

"It's too hard. The jungle is winning," Ethan thought as lay on his bed.

Then Joe came in. "What's the matter, little brother?"

"This jungle of stuff is ruining my life!"

Joe looked at the **clutter**. Thing were spread out everywhere. "You just need to get organized."

"But I don't know how!" Ethan said.

Joe beat his chest like Tarzan. "Big brother help little brother!"

"I'll help you get started," Joe said, and he found some paper. He wrote, "Goal: To get organized. Step one: Clean room. Step two: Make list of things to do. Step three: Write dates in planner. Step four: Make a schedule."

"I know it seems **ambitious**, but I'm sure you can do it," said Joe.

After Joe left, Ethan thought about how explorers make their way through dangerous places. "They travel through jungles. So I can do this," he thought.

Later, Ethan's mom came in. "This is a great start, Ethan! Do you want some help?"

They worked on the closet together. "This looks like a permission slip," his mom said, holding up a sheet of paper.

STOP AND CHECK

How did Joe help Ethan?

Chapter 4
BREAKING FREE!

The next morning, Ethan looked around his bedroom with **satisfaction**. It was no longer a jungle. His books were in the bookcase and his planner and a cup of pens and pencils sat on his desk. His things didn't fall out of the closet when he opened the door.

Ethan's calendar was pinned to the bulletin board. He had also written some dates in his planner.

"It was hard work to tame the jungle," Ethan thought, "but it was **worthwhile**. Now I know where things are."

Blake and Luis were at the bus stop when Ethan got there.

"Sorry, I forgot to remind you to bring your permission slip," Blake said.

"It's okay," Ethan grinned. "I've got it."

At school, Mr. Wong announced another group project. "Stay in the same groups you were in last time," he said.

Blake and Luis looked at each other, and Ethan wondered if they were worried. "But they don't know how organized I am now," Ethan thought.

"Let's **brainstorm** some ideas," Mr. Wong said. "Who has an idea?"

Ethan raised his hand, feeling as brave as a jungle explorer.

Later, Ethan volunteered to do his book presentation. "Well done!" said Mr. Wong.

After practice, Blake and Luis came over. The boys decided to play in the tree house.

"You'll need some food," Ethan's mom said. She handed Ethan a container of apples and bananas. "It's a jungle out there!"

Ethan hadn't played in the tree house in a long time. The branches had grown around it. The wind moved through the leaves and it sounded like an animal was up there, stalking its prey. Ethan **shuddered**. For a moment, he thought he saw the eyes of a tiger looking at him.

"Let's go!" Ethan said, and they charged into the jungle.

STOP AND CHECK

What are some things that show how Ethan has changed?

Summarize

Summarize *Clearing the Jungle*. Use key details from the story. Your graphic organizer may help you.

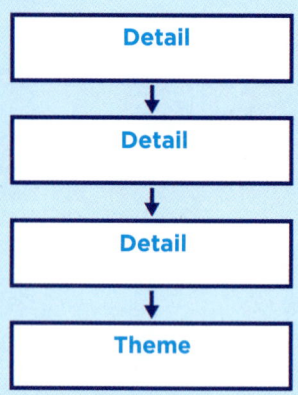

Text Evidence

1. What message is the author of *Clearing the Jungle* trying to tell readers? **THEME**

2. Find the word *slip* on page 7. What meanings can this word have? What clues helped you figure out the meaning in this sentence? **VOCABULARY**

3. Write about how Ethan's friends and his teacher change the way they act towards Ethan in Chapter 4. How does this change support the story's theme? **WRITE ABOUT READING**

CCSS Genre Poetry

Compare Texts
Read about a girl who sets a challenging goal.

My goal is simple. My goal is achievable.
    It concerns running
    It concerns running
and just for once—not coming in last.
Again.
My friends help me practice,
my mom helps me, too.
"Why don't you get up earlier?" she says,
"and I'll run with you."

So I make myself wake up—
before the sun throws back the covers
of the night and shines upon our world.
It doesn't seem like fun.
My mind tells my body,
"Give up now. It's not worth all this.
You'll never improve."
But even though my legs cry
even though my legs cry,
    I keep on!
    I keep on!

We run together. Mom breathes hard beside me.
I'm breathing hard, too,
and the wind's breath is on my face.
The lazy sun's rising at our backs, and suddenly
my legs stop cry-baby crying,
my feet search out the ground ahead.

Every day I run, sometimes with Mom,
sometimes with Jada and Leslie at school.
Never with my brother, who's far too cool
to run with his kid sister, who is always last.
Soon the day of the race arrives. Am I ready?

We line up, and there's the start.
My heart pumps, my legs pump,
my mind sings my running song—

> Run well, run strong!
> Run well, run strong!

Illustration: Steve Templer

Mom calls, "Go girl, go!"
I can hear Jordan, Leslie, and Jada yell, too,
as I take off down the course.

In a flash, like lightning, like lightning,
I dash past Megan and Alice, and others too!

    Is this really me?
Will this speed, this energy, last?
    Is this really me?
How long will I keep on
running this fast?

But I'm not past Caitlin, or Leanne—
they run so fast they almost fly—
they run, shoulders high.

Leanne breaks the tape, Caitlin comes second. Guess what? I bet no one would ever guess this—
I'm third for the very first time!
And, *at last*, most definitely, positively,
NOT LAST!

Make Connections

Why is it important for an athlete, such as a runner, to set a goal? **ESSENTIAL QUESTION**

How do family and friends help the characters reach their goals in each story? **TEXT TO TEXT**

Focus on Literary Elements

Rhyme and Repetition Poems do not always rhyme. And rhymes do not always come at the ends of lines. Free verse poems are like that. Rhymes can also be in the middle of a line. This can give the poem rhythm. Poets also use repetition, or repeated sounds or phrases. Repetition makes an important idea stand out.

Read and Find Look at page 17. In *Just for Once*, the phrase, "It concerns running," repeats in lines 2 and 3. The phrase, "I keep on!" repeats in the last two lines. The poet also includes rhymes in this poem. In lines 7 and 9, the words *too* and *you* are at the ends of the lines. In line 10, the rhyming words *make* and *wake* are in the middle. Look for more examples of repetition and rhymes.

Your Turn

Reread page 19 out loud with a partner. What phrases does the poet repeat? Why do you think the poet decided to use repetition? How did the repetition make you feel when you read the poem?